31 DAYS PROPHETIC TRANSFORMATION DEVOTIONAL

David S. Philemon

Royal Diadem Publishing Inc.

31 Days Prophetic Transformation Devotional
978-1-966141-28-0

For permissions, additional information, or bulk order inquiries, please contact the author.

Write:
Royal Diadem Publishing Inc.
4836 W. 13th Street, Cicero, IL 60804
1 (312) 970-0183

Unless otherwise indicated, all Scripture quotations in this volume are taken from the King James Version (KJV) and the New King James Version (NKJV) of the Holy Bible.

To the Almighty God, my foundation and ever-present help. I am grateful for Your boundless love and grace that sustain me daily. And to my mentor in ministry, Rev. George Izunwa, whose steadfast commitment to the call of God has deeply impacted my life. Your guidance and support have been invaluable, encouraging me to walk boldly in the path God has set before me. Thank you for your example and your heart for the Kingdom.

ACKNOWLEDGMENT

This book would not have been possible without the unwavering support, dedication, and talent of an extraordinary team. My deepest gratitude goes to each of you for your contributions, insights, and encouragement throughout this journey.

First and foremost, thank you to Rev. Mimi Philemon my dear wife, Rev. Shina Gentry, and and my assistant pastor Rev. Bright Amudoaghan for your incredible effort, encouragement, and belief in this project. Your support has been instrumental in bringing this vision to life.

To the dedicated leaders of Royal Diadem Publishing, Ide Imogie and Kishawna Bailey, I am immensely grateful for your belief in this project from the very beginning and for investing your time and energy into its development. Your creativity, dedication, and expertise have been the backbone of this endeavor.

I am especially grateful to the Royal Diadem Publishing team— Beulah Orogun, Emmanuella Ben-Eboh, Doyinsade Awodele, Kim Matthews, and Shante Gill, for your meticulous attention to detail, refining every page and ensuring that each word reflects our vision.

A heartfelt thank you to my family, friends, and colleagues whose unwavering support and belief in this project gave me the courage and strength to see it through.

Finally, thank you to all the readers and supporters who make this work meaningful. I am humbled and honored to share this journey with each of you.

With all my gratitude,
David Philemon

CONTENTS

INTRODUCTION

Welcome to the 31 Days Prophetic Transformation Devotional, a journey designed to deepen your relationship with God and unlock the life-transforming power of His Word in your life. In these pages, you will find insights and revelations that will guide you toward a more profound understanding of your identity in Christ and the promises He has for you.

Every day presents a new opportunity for transformation, growth, and discovery. As we embark on this journey together, we will explore the mysteries of the Kingdom of God, drawing on biblical truths that will inspire and challenge you to align your life with His divine purpose. This devotional is not merely a collection of thoughts but a prophetic declaration of what God desires to do in and through you during this season.

Throughout the next 31 days, you will encounter powerful scriptures, reflective insights, and heartfelt prayers that will empower you to embrace your God-given potential. Each day will encourage you to seek God earnestly, ensuring a genuine heart that loves Him and longs for His presence. As you engage with the material, expect to experience spiritual awakening, clarity, and direction in every area of your life.

Transformation begins with a decision to draw closer to God. With each devotion, you will uncover the keys to spiritual growth and the significance of maintaining a loving relationship with your Creator. You will learn how to navigate life's challenges with faith, understanding that God is at work, orchestrating your journey for His glory.

As you read and meditate on the teachings within this devotional, I invite you to approach it with an open heart, ready to receive the revelation and transformation God has in store for you. Let this time be marked by prayer, reflection, and a renewed commitment to pursuing His presence.

DAY 1

LET GOD ARISE –
OH GOD ARISE FOR
HIS CHURCH

Scripture Focus:
Luke 6:38 – "Give, and it shall be given unto you; good measure, pressed down, and shaken together, and running over, shall men give into your bosom. For with the same measure that ye mete withal it shall be measured to you again."*

As we enter into this day of prophetic transformation, we focus on allowing God to arise on behalf of His Church. The Church on Fire International, along with every believer, stands as a symbol of light in a dark world. We are reminded today that God has not allowed the enemy to laugh at His people or the Church. There is divine protection and favor over His Church and His people.

Reflecting on the testimony of Pastor E.W. Kenyon's church, where for 25 years, no one experienced death, we are reminded of the supernatural covering that God provides to those who walk in His principles. As children of God, we are called to live by these principles, for in them lies the key to victory and divine favor. When you don't know what to do, look for principles, you will never go wrong when you apply the principles of God's Word to your life.

God speaks to His people, sometimes through leadership and spiritual fathers. In one powerful encounter, I was directed by my spiritual father to attend a conference, and despite challenges, I obeyed. Through this obedience, the Lord used me to bless another pastor who had sacrificed everything to attend the same convention. It was through a simple act of obedience that God provided for him in a miraculous way.

This experience reinforces the importance of obedience in the life of a believer. When we pray and seek God's face, we must remember that He answers in His own unique way. As you pray, make this your declaration: "Lord, whenever You want to extend Your goodness to others, use me. And whenever You want to punish or criticize a servant of God, do not use me."

This is a powerful prayer of surrender and availability to the divine will of God. By aligning our hearts with God's purpose, we position ourselves to be instruments of His grace and love.

During a worship service, I had an encounter that shifted the course of my ministry. The power of God hit me, and I fell under His presence. In that moment, the Lord showed me a vision of my ministry expanding across North and South America. He declared that He had made me the father of these continents, and that through my obedience, I would see the manifestation of His promise.

The vision was clear, multitudes of people from different races and nations would come together under the banner of the Church. I saw leaders, front-liners, and champions rising from this ministry, destined to shape nations and impact the world for Christ. This vision was a confirmation of the mandate that God had given me, to raise a generation of leaders who would carry the gospel with power and authority.

This vision was not just for me, but for every believer who aligns themselves with the will of God. When God arises, He brings divine expansion, elevation, and influence. Today, as you pray, ask God to arise in your life, your ministry, and your family, bringing about His divine purpose and plans.

The Bible is filled with promises for those who walk in obedience to God. One such promise is found in Luke 6:38, which encourages us to give generously, with the assurance that God will give back to us in abundance. This principle of giving applies not only to finances but also to our time, talents, and spiritual gifts.

As you stand on God's promises, be confident that He will always reward your obedience. Just as He has blessed Church on Fire International with growth, protection, and influence, He will bless your life as you continue to walk in faith and obedience.

Prayer Points

1. Thanksgiving for God's Mercy and Protection:
Father, in the name of Jesus, we give You praise for Your mercies and compassion. Thank You for every testimony of Your goodness, protection, and preservation in our lives, families, and ministry. We thank You for the life You have given us and for every soul that has been saved and transformed through Church on Fire International. We return all the praise, honor, and glory to You, in Jesus' name.

2. Prayer for Divine Expansion and Influence:
Father, in the name of Jesus, by Your power and authority, we pray for divine expansion and influence for Church on Fire International and for every believer. Let Your anointing flow

through us, enabling us to touch lives, raise leaders, and impact nations for Your glory. We declare that we are vessels of Your grace, used to extend Your goodness to others.

3. Prayer for Obedience to God's Voice:
Father, help us to always be obedient to Your voice and to the guidance of spiritual leadership. We ask for the grace to follow Your instructions, even when it is difficult or inconvenient. Just as You used obedience to bring about provision and breakthrough in our lives, we ask that You continue to bless us as we walk in Your ways.

4. Prayer Against Slander and Division:
Lord, we declare that we will not be used for gossip, slander, or division within the body of Christ. We pray for unity and love to abound in the Church, and we bind every spirit of discord and strife. Let Your peace reign in every congregation and among every believer.

5. Prayer for Divine Revelation and Vision:
Father, we ask for divine revelation and vision for every believer. Just as You revealed the future of this ministry, we pray that You will open the eyes of Your people to see the plans and purposes You have for their lives. Let us walk in Your divine direction and fulfill the mandate You have given us.

DAY 2

THE POWER OF
DIVINE LEADERSHIP
AND EXCELLENCE

Scripture Focus:
"So the Lord alone did lead him, and there was no strange god with him. He made him ride on the high places of the earth, that he might eat the increase of the fields; and he made him to suck honey out of the rock, and oil out of the flinty rock."
Deuteronomy 32:12-13 (ERV)

We see from scripture that when God leads a people, as He did with Israel, He lifts them above the ordinary. Deuteronomy 32:12 tells us how God alone led Israel and kept them from serving strange gods. In return, He blessed them with abundance and prosperity. Similarly, we ask that God arises for the congregation of COFI, leading us to ride on the high places of the earth and to be blessed beyond measure in all areas of life. God is not only able to provide for our spiritual needs, but He is also committed to ensuring our success in every sphere.

Throughout history, many have failed not because of lack of effort but due to lack of divine direction. Without the voice of God, even the most talented and gifted individuals can lose their way. We learn from the story of Saul in 1 Samuel 28:5-6 that losing access to God's voice is worse than any physical imprisonment. Saul, though a king with immense power, could not hear from God, and that absence of divine guidance led to his downfall.

Today, many believers are trapped in a spiritual prison of confusion and stagnation because they lack a clear word from God. The noise of the world drowns out the still small voice of the Lord. But when we stay connected to God and His voice, He provides revelation, comfort, assurance, and direction.

Psalm 29:5-6 speaks about the voice of the Lord breaking the cedars and shaking the wilderness. The voice of God is powerful enough to break through any challenge, obstacle, or demonic barrier standing in your way. When God speaks, mountains move, and strongholds are broken. Today, we pray for the clarity of God's voice in the lives of the members of COFI, that no one will miss out on His divine instructions.

As we reflect on today's teaching, we recognize the value of obedience to God's instructions. Not everyone has the grace, unction, and power to follow God's voice as He leads, because it is not always easy. Jeremiah, though in prison for doing what was right, remained steadfast in obedience. His circumstances did not diminish his commitment to God. Similarly, we may encounter moments of adversity and trials, but those trials cannot override the importance of staying tuned to God's voice and obeying His word.

God's voice brings direction not only for us individually but also corporately as a church. COFI has a prophetic mandate to be a voice in the nations, taming the tormenting spirits in North America and beyond. Our church is not just an assembly, it is a movement that carries weight in the spiritual realm. God has placed us here to influence the nations, and our voice in the spirit realm carries the power to shift atmospheres, silence demonic forces, and break chains.

Today, we declare that the anointing for excellence will rest upon every member of Church on Fire International. We are not called to mediocrity; we are called to be the best in every field of human endeavor. Whether in politics, entertainment, ministry, or education, we ask God to raise leaders from among us who will represent His kingdom with dignity and honor. Just as Daniel was distinguished in Babylon for his wisdom and excellence, so too will members of COFI be distinguished in every sector they operate in.

We declare that COFI will be a breeding ground for world changers, and God will release the best of the best into our congregation. We pray for the emergence of the best politicians, doctors, engineers, lawyers, teachers, preachers, and entrepreneurs from our assembly. The anointing of leadership, innovation, and creativity will be upon us as we take territories and expand the kingdom of God.

The word of God assures us in Deuteronomy 32:12-14 that God led His people to ride on the high places of the earth and provided them with the best of the land. They ate the finest wheat and drank honey from the rock. Likewise, we decree that every member of COFI will experience the best that God has to offer. We will not settle for less, for we serve a God who gives exceedingly and abundantly above all we can ask or think.

Prayer Points

1: Thanksgiving for Divine Direction and Leadership

DAY 3

OBEDIENCE AND THE GRACE TO DO GOD'S WILL

Scripture Focus:
"For it is God who works in you both to will and to do for His good pleasure." Philippians 2:13

Many times, obeying the desires of God can seem difficult because they often go beyond human logic and understanding. It is natural to question or struggle with things that do not make immediate sense, but the reality is that God operates beyond the realm of our reasoning.

Romans 8:6 tells us that carnality, living by our senses and human logic, makes it difficult to comprehend spiritual things. Carnality often resists the will of God, causing us to rely on our own intelligence, which can be misleading. However, when we allow God's revelation to guide us, He gives us the grace to both understand and act on His will.

Take the example of Joseph in Genesis 50:20, where his family could not understand God's hand in his situation because they viewed things through a carnal lens. Yet, God had a bigger plan in store. Likewise, we must be open to the work of the Holy Spirit in our lives to remove spiritual blindness, granting us the eyes to see God's higher purposes.

When God instructs us, He doesn't leave us to figure it out on our own. He provides grace to obey. Philippians 2:13 reminds us that God not only works in us to desire His will, but also gives us the ability to carry it out. It is through faith that we grow this grace. As Romans 10:17 says, "Faith comes by hearing, and hearing by the word of God." As we immerse ourselves in God's word, our faith grows, and with it, our grace to follow through on what God asks of us.

There will be moments in life when obeying God won't make sense to the world, and even our loved ones may struggle to understand. But we must remain steadfast, knowing that God sees everything, and He rewards faithfulness.

Reflection

Is there an area in your life where God is asking you to obey Him, but it seems illogical or difficult? Trust in His grace to help you follow through. Remember that God will provide the strength and faith needed to fulfill His good pleasure in your life. Pray for the salvation and transformation of your loved ones, that they too may receive spiritual sight and be willing to do the will of God.

Prayer

Father, in the name of Jesus, we thank You for Your grace and mercy that enable us to do Your will. We give You praise for the past few days of this devotional, and we honor You for everyone participating, both in person and online. Lord, we thank You for Your faithfulness in supplying us with the desire and the ability to obey You. We plead the blood of Jesus against any interference in our obedience and answers. Thank You for Your grace that sustains us and helps us grow in faith. Take all the glory, Lord, in Jesus' mighty name. Amen.

DAY 4

WALKING IN THE FULLNESS OF SPIRITUAL POWER AND AUTHORITY

Scripture Focus:
"But you shall receive power when the Holy Spirit has come upon you; and you shall be witnesses to Me in Jerusalem, and in all Judea and Samaria, and to the end of the earth." – Acts 1:8

In the kingdom of God, power is essential for walking in dominion and fulfilling the purpose of God on earth. Without spiritual power, we become vulnerable, living a life without authority, unable to overcome the forces that oppose us. Power is what sets believers apart and grants us the ability to overturn the plans of the enemy.

As believers, we are called to manifest the glory of both the former and the latter house, walking in the fullness of spiritual power and authority that comes through the Holy Spirit. We are equipped with the power to heal the sick, cast out demons, and perform signs and wonders in the name of Jesus. Just as Moses' rod swallowed the rods of the magicians in Pharaoh's court (Exodus 7:12), so too does the power of God within us neutralize and destroy every evil projection against us.

The Bible teaches us that the Spirit and the powers of the world to come are available to those who hunger and thirst for them. As we grow in spiritual authority, even the presence of witches, wizards, and those with satanic powers will melt in the presence of the glory of God in us. This is the power that not only protects us but also brings about the manifestation of miracles and the advancement of God's kingdom.

Reflection

Are you walking in the fullness of the spiritual authority available to you as a believer? If not, now is the time to seek God for an outpouring of His power. The same power that raised Jesus from the dead is available to us, but we must be willing to pray, praise, and seek the face of God for its full manifestation in our lives. Remember, without power, we are powerless in the face of the enemy, but with God's power, we are more than conquerors.

Prayer

Father, in the name of Jesus, I receive Your great power and the powers of the world to come. I receive the power to heal the sick, raise the dead, cast out devils, and destroy demonic entities. Lord, I thank You for granting me the power to walk in authority, dominion, and spiritual wealth. I receive Your power to fully represent You by manifesting great miracles, signs, and wonders in my generation. Thank You, Lord, for making me a carrier of Your glory and power. I will walk in this power and change my world for Your kingdom, in Jesus' name. Amen.

DAY 5

FULL MANIFESTATION OF FINANCIAL GLORY

Scripture Reference: Zechariah 1:17 (KJV) "My cities through prosperity shall yet be spread abroad; and the Lord shall yet comfort Zion, and shall yet choose Jerusalem.

Theme: Breaking Financial Warfare And Unlocking Divine Wealth

Today's devotional focus is on the full manifestation of financial glory and the breaking of any warfare that has kept finances away from God's people. For too long, many have faced financial battles that have prevented them from walking in the abundance and prosperity that God desires for them. The Lord, in His mercy, is declaring that the warfare keeping your finances bound shall be silenced this week, in the name of Jesus!

God is calling His people to a higher level of financial glory, but the pathway to that glory is not without its challenges. Today is a day of wealth, but it is also a day of warfare. There is an indignation that has been determined by the Lord. The wicked will stop at nothing in their pursuit to keep God's people in lack, but the Lord is determined to overthrow the wicked. However, in the midst of this, there is also a time of testing, a season where God is remodeling and reshaping His people.

Wealth, in the middle of spiritual warfare, can be meaningless without the right preparation. The Lord has revealed that war is coming, and with it, a purging of the wicked. But in this purging, there will be a manifestation of financial glory for those who have remained faithful, obedient, and aligned with His covenant.

In the spirit, there has been a revelation of chaos and destruction. The entire nation is covered in blood, and there is a great deal of suffering. This is not the desire of the Lord, but it is a necessary part of His plan to overthrow the wicked. As believers, we must prepare for this time by staying connected to the covenant we have with God. The righteous will be preserved in the midst of the storm, but we must ensure that our hearts and lives are aligned with His will.

What if this time of testing comes, and it takes many by surprise? What if those who have shouted, "I will live and not die," are taken unprepared? The Lord is calling His people to wake up and be vigilant in this season. There is a lying spirit at work, seeking to deceive and make light of God's instructions. But the time has come for the determined indignation of the Lord to purify His people and silence the warfare over their finances.

God is speaking clearly: "My people are not sold out to Me." The Lord is looking for those who are willing to give their time, their resources, and their lives fully to His service. He does not need our money, but we must prove who we worship by where we invest our resources. Many of us have been too casual in our commitment, offering only partial obedience. The time for half-hearted devotion is over.

The Lord is calling us to radical obedience, especially in the area of our finances. Those who are willing to sacrifice, who are willing to give even when it seems difficult, will be the ones who see the full manifestation of financial glory. Just as the wicked are willing to sacrifice everything for their agenda, God's people must be willing to do the same for His kingdom.

In this season, God is positioning His people to walk in financial abundance, but He is also building us up spiritually so that the wealth He entrusts to us does not destroy us. Many believers are not yet ready for the level of wealth that God desires to release, because their hearts have not been fully transformed.

Jeroboam, a servant of Solomon, is a biblical example of someone who was given great authority and wealth, but his heart was not transformed. He led Israel into idolatry and built altars for idols, leading the people astray (1 Kings 12:28,). This shows the danger of untransformed hearts handling wealth. If God were to give some of us the level of prosperity we desire right now, it would lead to spiritual destruction because we have not yet been fully prepared.

The Lord is teaching us that the foundation for financial glory is total surrender to Him. When we give God our hearts, our time, our obedience, and our resources, He will entrust us with wealth that will not only bless us but will also spread His kingdom and bring comfort to His people.

Prayer Points

1. Breaking Financial Warfare:
Father, in the name of Jesus, by Your power and authority, I declare that every warfare that has kept my finances bound is silenced this week. I break free from every financial stronghold and declare

that my wealth is being released from the enemy's grip.

2. Covenant of Financial Glory:
Lord, I enter into a new level of covenant with You. I give You my heart, my mind, my time, and my resources. I commit to radical obedience, knowing that as I give to Your kingdom, You will pour out financial glory upon my life.

3. Divine Wealth Transfer:
Father, I declare that the wealth of the wicked is being transferred to the righteous. I receive the financial glory that has been prepared for me, and I will use it to advance Your kingdom and bless others.

4. Purification for Financial Abundance:
Lord, purify my heart. Prepare me for the financial abundance You are about to release. Transform my mind and align my heart with Your will, so that I can handle the wealth You are entrusting to me without falling into temptation or idolatry.

5. Supernatural Increase:
Father, I thank You for supernatural increase in every area of my life. I declare that as I sow into Your kingdom, You are multiplying my resources and giving me the power to create wealth.

Today, declare over your life: "I am a vessel for God's financial glory. I will walk in wealth and abundance, and I will use my resources to advance God's kingdom."

DAY 6

EMBRACING
THE POWER OF
GOD'S MERCY

Scriptural Focus:
Lamentations 3:22-23 (KJV) declares, "It is of the Lord's mercies that we are not consumed, because His compassions fail not. They are new every morning: great is Thy faithfulness"

The mercies of God are vast and beyond human comprehension. They are the very force that restrains destruction and ushers us into His protective embrace. While the world may be in turmoil, and judgment may seem imminent, there is hope, hope in the mercy of God. As believers, we are called to recognize His mercies and position ourselves to receive them.

Lamentations 3:22-23 (KJV) declares, "It is of the Lord's mercies that we are not consumed, because His compassions fail not. They are new every morning: great is Thy faithfulness." Today, as we enter into this day of transformation, let us acknowledge the mercies of God that have kept us safe and provided healing for our spirits, minds, and bodies.

Though destruction may loom, we have a ray of hope, God's mercy. This mercy not only shields us from judgment but also restores what has been broken. As we cry out for His mercy today, let us do so with hearts of humility and faith, knowing that He is ready to extend His compassionate hand toward us.

What Are The Mercies Of God?

1. The Mercies of God as a Restraint Against Destruction: The mercy of God prevents the full force of destruction from falling upon us. Even when the wicked sow seeds of evil, the mercies of God protect His people. As Lamentations 3:22 says, it is by His mercy that we are not consumed. His mercy is our ark of safety in times of trouble, a shield that confounds even the angels and the forces of darkness.

2. The Mercies of God as a Restorer: Mercy doesn't just prevent judgment, it heals and restores. Whether we need healing in our physical bodies, emotional wounds, or spiritual brokenness, the mercy of God brings complete restoration. Jeremiah 30:17-19 reminds us that God promises to restore health and heal our wounds. Through His mercy, we are made whole.

3. The Mercies of God as Compassion: Compassion, in the biblical sense, is more than pity. It's empathy, a deep, personal concern for our weaknesses and limitations. God's mercy means He knows we cannot meet His standards on our own, so He provides the grace we need to overcome and flourish.

The Key To Receiving God's Mercy

To receive God's mercy, we must:

1. Acknowledge Its Existence: Many believers assume that mercy is only for sinners, but even the righteous need mercy daily. Without God's mercy, we would all be consumed. We must recognize that His mercy is essential for our continued protection and restoration.

2. Acknowledge Our Need for It: No matter how righteous we may be, we are still in need of God's mercy. Romans 9:15-16 reminds us that mercy is not something we earn but something God chooses to give. Like Bartimaeus, we must cry out to Jesus, knowing that mercy is the key to our deliverance.

3. Sow the Seed of Mercy: Matthew 5:7 declares, "Blessed are the merciful, for they shall obtain mercy." We cannot expect to receive mercy if we are not willing to extend it to others. As we show mercy, we position ourselves to receive even more of God's abundant grace.

Activating God's Mercy Through Prayer and Worship

Mercy must be activated through prayer, fasting, and worship. Every time we humble ourselves before God, acknowledging our dependence on His mercy, we unlock its power over our lives. As 2 Chronicles 20:21 shows, the weapon of mercy can overturn the plans of the enemy.

As we pray today, let us invite God's mercy into every area of our lives. Mercy will remove the judgment, destruction, and condemnation we deserve. Whether it's healing from physical illness, restoration of broken relationships, or deliverance from financial difficulties, the cry of mercy is one God cannot resist.

Prayer Points

1. Recognizing His Mercies: Lord, we thank You for Your mercy

that has kept us from being consumed. We acknowledge our need for Your mercy every day. Without it, we are lost. Pour out Your mercy upon us and restore every broken area in our lives.

2. Healing and Restoration: Father, we cry out for Your mercy to heal every spiritual, physical, emotional, and relational wound in our lives. Heal us from the inside out, and let Your mercy bring complete restoration. Jeremiah 30:17-19 promises that You will restore health to us and heal our wounds. We claim that healing now in Jesus' name.

3. Protection From Destruction: God, we recognize that without Your mercy, destruction would be inevitable. But today, we stand under the covering of Your mercy. Protect us from every form of judgment and warfare. Let Your mercy be our shield, and let every plan of the enemy be overturned by Your grace.

DAY 7

THE POWER OF GOD'S MERCY AND TIMING

Scripture Reading: 2 Corinthians 6:2 (TLB)
"For God says, 'At just the right time, I heard you. On the day of salvation, I helped you.' Indeed, the 'right time' is now. Today is the day of salvation."

In our journey of faith, one profound truth stands out: God's mercy is the key to our divine breakthrough. The scriptures remind us in Lamentations 3:22-23 that "it is of the Lord's mercies that we are not consumed." This promise offers us hope amidst the chaos, especially in times when it seems like everything is falling apart.

Mercy is more than just forgiveness; it is the active love of God that shields us from destruction. Just as God demonstrated mercy throughout biblical history, He is extending that same mercy to us today. It is important to recognize that mercy is available not just for sinners but for every believer. When we acknowledge our need for God's mercy, we position ourselves for divine intervention.

The Dynamics of Timing
The entrance of God's light brings clarity, but the manifestation of His Word often takes time. Just as a seed must be planted, watered, and cultivated before it produces fruit, so too must we wait on the Lord to fulfill His promises. Ephesians 3:20 (TLB) reassures us that the power of God works within us before it manifests outwardly. We must remain patient, trusting that God's timing is perfect.

To receive God's mercy, we must actively acknowledge its presence in our lives. This involves recognizing the moments when we fall short and understanding that we need His compassion to cover us. Matthew 5:7 reminds us, "Blessed are the merciful, for they shall obtain mercy."

In our prayers, let us declare our dependence on God's mercy. As we pray today, we will ask for His mercy to envelop us and grant us the patience to wait for our breakthroughs. Just like Hannah, who persevered in prayer, we must also be diligent. Hannah's character was tested before her divine visitation, revealing that our readiness to receive God's blessings is often gauged by our attitude in times of waiting.

Reflection

Take a moment today to meditate on the times God has shown you mercy. Write them down as a reminder of His faithfulness and a testament to His unfailing love. Allow this reflection to encourage you in the moments when you feel overwhelmed, knowing that today is your day for transformation.

Prayer Points

1. Acknowledge His Mercies: Father, I recognize Your mercy in my life. Thank You for shielding me from the judgment I deserve.

Help me to be aware of Your grace at work.

2. Activate Divine Timing: Lord, I pray for the wisdom to understand Your timing. As I await Your promises, let me remain steadfast in faith, trusting that You are orchestrating everything for my good.

3. Guard My Heart: Lord, help me to maintain a heart of gratitude and humility. Let me not despise those You send to bless me, but let me see You in them.

4. Let Mercy Speak: May the cry of mercy resonate within me, drawing me closer to Your healing and restoration in every area of my life.

DAY 8

THE MYSTERY OF OBEDIENCE AND DIVINE REWARD

Scripture Focus:
"Call to Me, and I will answer you, and show you great and mighty things, which you do not know." – Jeremiah 33:3

As we walk in faith, it is essential to recognize the vital role that obedience plays in our relationship with God. Our willingness to do His will is not merely an act of compliance; it is a profound expression of our love for Him and a reflection of our understanding of His character. Yet, many believers remain unrewarded in their efforts because they fulfill God's will with grumbling and murmuring instead of with joy and gratitude. Such an attitude can undermine the blessings God desires to pour out upon us.

Understanding God's will is a grace we must seek daily. It doesn't matter how close we may feel to God; we should continually pray for the ability to know, comprehend, interpret, and carry out His will with graciousness. This prayer for grace should be a priority in our lives, as it opens our hearts to receive divine insights and guidance.

The truth is, knowing God's will can be a double-edged sword. When we are aware of His intentions for our lives, it becomes crucial that we respond appropriately. The temptation to brag about our spiritual knowledge can lead to spiritual pride, which in turn hinders our relationship with God. This pride can diminish our capacity to engage effectively in the invisible warfare that surrounds us. Satan does not fear our knowledge alone; he fears our sincere desire to please God. If he cannot corrupt our desire to serve God with feelings of discontent, he may resort to launching inexplicable attacks against us.

Yet, we are not left defenseless. The key to overcoming these challenges lies not in our own strength but in the grace that God provides. When we embrace humility and seek His power, we find the strength to withstand every temptation and battle that comes our way. Remember that obedience is not about our capabilities; it is about the grace that empowers us to fulfill His will.

Reflect on your life: Are you walking according to God's will? Are you fulfilling His purpose with a grateful heart, or are you allowing discouragement, pride, and grumbling to overshadow your commitment? The presence of God in our lives and our dedication to living according to His principles are crucial for reflecting His glory. If our salvation does not manifest in our families and communities, we risk allowing the enemy to insult our faith and witness. The enemy may attempt to convince us that we are worth nothing, but we must prove him wrong through our obedience and the visible fruits of our faith.

Reflection

This day is a day of mysteries, a time to seek understanding and revelation from God. Engage with the Spirit and inquire about the mysteries of obedience and the blessings of aligning with His will. Remember that every effort you make to serve Him is seen, and God does not forget those who earnestly seek Him. Your life, intertwined with God's principles, has the potential to become a powerful testament to His grace and glory.

Prayer

Heavenly Father, I come before You today with a heart full of gratitude. Thank You for the privilege of knowing Your will and understanding Your ways. I humbly ask for the grace to align with Your purpose and to exercise Your will with joy and thankfulness. Help me resist the temptation to grumble or murmur as I walk in obedience. May I never forget that my efforts to serve You are seen and rewarded by You? Lord, I desire to be a vessel of Your glory, reflecting Your love and power in all I do. Let the mysteries of Your kingdom unfold in my life as I seek to honor You. Strengthen my heart, open my eyes, and attune my ears to Your voice. In Jesus' name, I pray. Amen.

DAY 9

BREAKING CYCLES AND SHIFTING SEASONS

S cripture Focus:
"Call to Me, and I will answer you and show you great and mighty things, which you do not know." – Jeremiah 33:3

In the spirit of intercession, we stand today to break every cycle of negativity that may have encamped upon our lives and families. We declare that every demonic activity that has sought to hinder our progress and deliverance is destroyed in the name of Jesus. Let deliverance fall upon every household, every family, everyone represented, and particularly upon North America and Church On Fire International. As we pray, let us remember that when we lift our voices in praise and worship, we invite the presence of God to manifest His glory among us.

The Lord will rise upon us, and His glory will be seen in our midst. It is a day of supernatural intervention. Just as 2 Chronicles 20:22 tells us that when the people sang and praised God, He sent ambushments against their enemies, we too can expect that as we worship, God is moving to deliver us from every form of bondage.

Over the next few days, let healing fall like fire upon every form of sickness and affliction among us. Let it come as rain, refreshing our people's lives and revealing our God's might and glory. We declare favor like fire over Church On Fire International, igniting an extraordinary wave of miracles, signs, wonders, healing, and restoration. Let this ultimate favor, the regulator of greatness, grace, speed, and wealth, fall upon us as we unite, O God, arise, and let Your enemies be scattered!

Reflection

As we pray today, let us be mindful that our redemptive package includes the promise that everything should go right in our lives. We must not allow any room for disorder. Challenges may arise, but remember that tests will lead us to testimonies, not years later, but immediately.

The miracles of Jesus exemplify the mindset of God; they teach us that our troubles are often less significant than we perceive. In 1 Peter 5:10, we are reminded that after we have suffered for a little while, God Himself will perfect, establish, strengthen, and settle us. It is crucial to recognize that staying fixated on "what is wrong" can trap us in a cycle of despair. If your heart is prepared for answers, be assured that God will respond swiftly. Delays in receiving answers often stem from a lack of readiness in our hearts. When God sees a heart ready to receive, He answers by fire.

Prayer

Heavenly Father, I come before You with a heart longing for

transformation. I acknowledge my need for Your guidance as I navigate the cycles in my life. Help me to break free from every negative cycle that has held me captive. I pray for a heart ready to receive Your answers and ask for Your mercy to envelop my life and those around me. Let the blood of Jesus cleanse me from all guilt and shame, and may Your mercy overflow upon Church On Fire International.

DAY 10

THE POWER OF INTERCESSION AND SPIRITUAL VIGILANCE

Scripture Reading: Genesis 18:32, Matthew 21:28-31

As we enter Day 10 of our 31 Days Prophetic Transformation, we are reminded of the immense power of intercession and our responsibility as spiritual gatekeepers. In Genesis 18:32, God reveals to Abraham the potential for salvation through the intercession of the righteous: "If I find ten righteous men." This underscores the significant impact our prayers can have on our communities and nations.

Intercession is not merely a religious duty but a profound privilege. When we stand in the gap for others, we become instruments of God's mercy and grace. Matthew 21:28-31 illustrates three responses to God's call: some may say "no" but eventually act, others may agree but fail to follow through, while the genuinely committed say, "Yes, Lord, I am available." We must align our spirits, minds, and bodies to be fully present in our intercessory roles. God desires our active participation to manifest His glory on earth.

We must take pride in our access to spiritual revelations in our journey. These insights enable us to understand God's instructions for us and the urgency of our intercession. The depth of our commitment today will determine the grace we experience tomorrow. Though some may sleep through this transformative process, those awake will find themselves in realms of power, grace, and glory that they cannot yet comprehend.

As we pray and intercede, we must remain spiritually vigilant. Many face battles without recognizing the premonitions that God provides to prepare us. Slumbering, physically and spiritually, hinders our ability to receive vital instructions from God. Just as Job experienced distraction from his righteousness, we too may miss critical moments of divine guidance if we are not alert.

No battle arises without a warning. The true challenge is our ability to recognize and act upon these warnings. Instruction is our safeguard against the pitfalls of life. When we miss our assigned seasons to tackle challenges, we must be ready to respond quickly lest we miss the opportunity for a breakthrough. Spiritual battles demand our utmost attention and preparation.

God speaks to us, yet many struggle to hear. As Job 33:12-18 reminds us, God seals instruction within us, but we must combat the spirit of slumbering that seeks to close our eyes to His voice. Each prophecy carries both instruction and the potential for opposition. Our responsibility is to wage warfare over the prophetic words spoken into our lives, safeguarding them from the enemy's tactics.

As we engage in this period of intense prayer, let us understand that the power of our prayers can reshape destinies. Just as

God spared cities through the intercession of a few righteous individuals, our faithful prayers can influence our generation. God is always seeking hearts that are ready to hear and respond to His whispers.

Prayer is our pathway to stability. Psalm 27:4-8 emphasizes the importance of being anchored in God. When we build our lives on the solid rock of faith, we become resistant to the winds of adversity. A heart that is open and receptive to God will naturally respond to His call. Conversely, a heart polluted with sin and distractions will struggle to approach Him.

We are called not to be passive observers but active partners in God's mission. Our willingness to engage in prayer and intercession is a testament to our desire for spiritual growth and understanding. Many seek natural blessings but overlook the spiritual power that sustains them. Nurturing our spiritual lives is essential so that when challenges arise, we are firmly anchored in God's promises.

Prayer Points

1. Lord, awaken my spirit to recognize the power of intercession in my life.
2. Help me to remain vigilant and attentive to Your voice and instructions.
3. May my prayers bring healing and restoration to my community and beyond.
4. Lord, remove any distractions that hinder my ability to hear You clearly.
5. Fill me with a heart eager to do Your will and serve Your Kingdom.

DAY 11

THE POWER
OF LANGUAGE
IN SPIRITUAL
TRANSFORMATION

Scripture Reading: Genesis 10:4-5, 32; Acts 2:4

After the flood, God populated the earth through Noah's sons, each speaking a distinct language. This reveals that communication is not just a means of expressing thoughts but a powerful tool that shapes nations and influences destinies. When God's people communicate His language, they wield incredible power to affect change.

Satan has mastered the art of manipulation through language. When miscommunication occurs, it often leads to destruction.

We must understand that there are only two languages on this earth: the language of God and the language of the devil. The language of God speaks of His goodness, righteousness, and love, while the language of the devil conveys wickedness, jealousy, and despair. In a world where the devil's language predominates, it is crucial for us, as believers, to recognize the need to speak God's language in our families, communities, and nations.

Jacob and Esau, although individuals, represented entire nations. Genesis 25:23 reminds us that our visions can have a generational impact. God is actively seeking individuals who understand and communicate His language. When we align our words and actions with God's thoughts, we can effectively represent Him in a world longing for truth and light.

In Acts 2:4, we see the transformative power of the Holy Spirit as He alters the disciples' language. The Spirit empowers us to communicate God's message, enabling us to influence those around us. We must allow the Holy Spirit to guide our speech and actions to fill the earth with God's glory. We must become vessels through which God's language can flow.

Sometimes, communicating God's language requires forceful action. We may need to confront the lies and deceptions that saturate our communities. As we engage in prayer, we speak the language of God, breaking down barriers and redefining narratives that do not align with His will. This spiritual warfare is necessary to remove contradictory languages distorting God's truth.

The more we engage with God's language, the more we will see transformation. If Christians take their rightful place, the entire earth can resonate with a new language. By speaking the language of God, we create an environment where righteousness, peace, love, and joy can flourish. Our conversations should reflect these virtues, influencing those around us and drawing them closer to God.

However, we must acknowledge that there are times when God may need to "flush out" contradictory languages to establish His voice. Before Noah's flood, the world was rife with evil (Genesis 6:5), leading to divine intervention. Similarly, in Genesis 11:1, the lack of alignment with God's language resulted in confusion and division among people. God scattered the nations to prevent the unity of wickedness, illustrating the necessity of divine oversight in our communication.

Nations today still struggle with the consequences of speaking the wrong language. For instance, in some countries, violence and chaos dominate the conversation, rooted in the enemy's desire to sow discord. The devil seeks to divide communities, making it imperative for us to stand firm in the language of God. We must be vigilant against the influences that cause division and confusion among God's people.

Nimrod, a figure from Scripture, serves as a warning. Though he possessed great power, it ultimately led him to oppose God. An evil spirit influenced him, and his ambition led to his downfall. Just as God intervened in Nimrod's time, He will address any misalignment in our speech today. We must ensure that we are not unwittingly participating in the enemy's schemes by speaking a language contrary to God's.

As we go out today, let us commit to understanding and speaking the language of God. Our words carry weight and can potentially shape the atmosphere around us. We can counter the prevailing darkness by immersing ourselves in God's thoughts and communicating His truth. Together, let us rise as ambassadors of His kingdom, influencing our families, communities, and nations with the glorious language of God.

Prayer Points

1. Lord, help me to recognize and speak Your language in my daily

interactions.

2. May Your Holy Spirit guide my words and actions to reflect Your truth.

3. Give me the strength to confront and dismantle the language of the enemy in my community.

4. Teach me to communicate love, peace, and righteousness in all I do.

5. Empower me to be a vessel through which Your glory fills the earth.

DAY 12

THE IMPACT OF FAITH IN OUR LIVES

Scripture Reading: Hebrews 11:1-2, James 1:5

Faith is the foundation of our relationship with God and the key to unlocking His promises. Hebrews 11:1 reminds us that "faith is the substance of things hoped for, the evidence of things not seen." This foundational truth reinforces the importance of living by faith, even in times of uncertainty.

Genuine faith is not merely a passive belief; it requires action. It moves us out of our comfort zones, trusting God's character and promises. When we exercise faith, we demonstrate our trust in God's sovereignty, which empowers us to navigate life's challenges confidently. James 1:5 encourages us to seek wisdom from God, assuring us that He generously gives to all without finding fault. This wisdom is essential as we align our actions with our faith.

Cconsider the story of Abraham, who is often hailed as the father of faith. In Genesis 12, he obeyed God's call to leave his homeland without knowing his destination. Abraham's faith led him to incredible blessings and covenant promises. Likewise, our faith should compel us to respond to God's leading, regardless of how daunting the journey may seem. When we act in faith, we allow God to move powerfully in our lives and circumstances.

Faith does not eliminate doubt, but it empowers us to overcome it. When we face obstacles, succumbing to fear and uncertainty is easy. However, we must remind ourselves that faith thrives amid challenges. Just as a seed grows in darkness before it breaks through the soil, our faith can flourish in trials. Through these moments of struggle, we experience growth, maturity, and deeper intimacy with God.

Our journey of faith is not meant to be solitary. We are called to support one another within the Body of Christ. Hebrews 10:24-25 encourages us to consider how we may spur one another toward love and good deeds, not giving up a meeting. Engaging with fellow believers fosters accountability, encouragement, and growth in our faith journeys. Together, we can share testimonies of God's faithfulness, which inspires and strengthens our collective faith.

As we go out today, let us reaffirm our commitment to live by faith. We can face the future with hope and assurance when we trust in God's promises. Our faith is not just for our benefit but a beacon of hope for others watching our lives. Let us be living testimonies of God's faithfulness, demonstrating the transformative power of faith in our everyday lives.

Prayer Points

1. Lord, strengthen my faith and help me to trust You more deeply.
2. Grant me the wisdom to seek Your guidance in all areas of my life.
3. May my faith inspire others to seek You and experience Your goodness.
4. Help me to overcome doubt and fear, reminding me of Your faithfulness.

5. Surround me with a community of believers encouraging and uplifting my faith journey.

DAY 13

THE POWER OF CORPORATE ANOINTING

Scripture Reading: Deuteronomy 32:30 (TLB)

The principle of togetherness in prayer and worship cannot be overstated. When we unite our voices and hearts in prayer, we connect in the spirit realm, unlocking an anointing that can dismantle challenges and bring about transformation. The collaboration of corporate prayer amplifies our spiritual influence, allowing us to overcome obstacles that may seem insurmountable.

The power of corporate anointing stems from the collective faith and intention of believers. Just as Deuteronomy 32:30 reminds us of the strength found in unity, we see this principle illustrated throughout Scripture. In 1 Chronicles 11:4-6, David, united with his men, faced the Jebusites to capture Jerusalem. His determination to seize the city was driven by personal ambition and a prophetic understanding of its future significance. His efforts earned him a unique place in God's plan and a special favor in Heaven.

This understanding highlights that our actions in unity can have far-reaching implications, shaping not only our destinies but also generations to come. God does not get excited merely by our financial welfare or material gain; instead, He delights in our ability to align with His eternal purpose. We invite God's anointing into our lives and communities when we engage in collective prayers, seeking His will and understanding our contributions.

As we embrace this corporate anointing, we must also recognize the call to engage in spiritual warfare. Isaiah 28:5-6 emphasizes the necessity of being strong in the Spirit. We cannot afford to be passive in our faith; we must intentionally confront the darkness that seeks to overshadow our lives and those around us. The enemy often employs indirect tactics to catch us off guard, targeting our families and communities with sorrow and strife.

In the face of these challenges, we are called to stand firm, armed with the knowledge that we carry a divine mantle. This mantle empowers us to wage war against the forces of darkness. As we pray today, we create a spiritual force to dismantle the enemy's plans. We must remember that God is helping us recreate and redefine the spiritual atmosphere over our lives during this season of prophetic transformation.

The most insidious battles we face are often the ones we cannot see. Indirect warfare can manifest in our relationships, workplaces, and families. As believers, we must be vigilant and proactive, praying to counter these attacks. 2 Kings 6:9-10 shows how the Lord alerts us to the enemy's schemes, enabling us to respond in prayer and declare victory before the battles arise.

As we journey through these 31 days, let us be mindful of the weight our prayers carry. When we gather in faith, our voices resonate in the heavenly realms, and the anointing is released to confront every challenge we face.

A crucial aspect of this journey is recognizing and addressing spiritual abortions, those moments when we lose zeal and focus just as we are on the brink of a breakthrough. Many have experienced the fire of God's presence only to become distracted and discouraged when challenges arise. This week, we declare a restoration of every lost opportunity and destiny.

Revelation 12:5-9 reminds us that God's power is at work even when we feel under siege. As we pray, we affirm that this week marks a decisive turning point in our spiritual journeys. The dragon and all his cohorts will lose their grip over our lives, families, and communities.

Prayer Points

1. Lord, help me to understand the power of corporate anointing and how to utilize it effectively in prayer.
2. May I be vigilant against indirect warfare and stand firm in faith to protect my family and community.
3. I declare restoration for every spiritual abortion in my life; may I receive back every lost destiny.
4. Empower me to be an agent of change in my community through persistent prayer and action.
5. Let every battle I face lead to the enemy's defeat and the advancement of Your Kingdom.

DAY 14

PRAYING AGAINST THE WINDS OF ADVERSITY

Scripture Reference: Job 1:17-21 (TLB), Mark 4:37

As we continue our journey in this 31-Day Prophetic Transformation Devotional, today we focus on the winds of adversity that seek to disrupt our peace and steal our joy. Just as Job faced calamity through the unseen winds of the spirit realm, we, too, must be vigilant against the spiritual forces that threaten to undermine our faith and purpose. The enemy desires to take advantage of our weaknesses and create chaos.

Winds in the spiritual realm often symbolize spirits or forces that can influence our circumstances. Job's story reveals that these winds can come suddenly without warning, leading to significant trials and tribulations. The Hebrew word for "wind," "Ruach," also translates to "spirit," emphasizing the spiritual implications behind these seemingly natural occurrences.

When the winds of disaster blow, they can wreak havoc on our health, finances, relationships, and even our spiritual walk. Just as the Israelites were intimidated by the Anakims and desired to return to bondage (Numbers 13:33), we too can fall victim to fear and discouragement when faced with overwhelming challenges.

In the face of these adversities, we must rise with declarations of faith. As you read this, proclaim: "Nothing bad will ever happen to me." Let this declaration resonate in your spirit, countering every lie of the enemy. A focused life, rooted in God's truth, will not succumb to the distractions that the enemy throws our way.

We must also recognize that the enemy's attacks often target those who carry spiritual authority within their families. If you stand in the gap for your loved ones, you may experience indirect warfare. Satan's goal is to undermine your effectiveness and weaken the spiritual defenses of those around you.

Our possessions, health, dreams, and relationships are not just material; they encompass our spiritual inheritance. When the enemy steals our focus, he jeopardizes our ability to manifest the greatness God has placed within us. A distracted life is a vulnerable life. We must fight to maintain our focus and not allow the winds of adversity to derail us from our God-given purpose.

Job faced an attack that sought to strip him of everything he held dear, and we must be prepared to fight against similar forces. Remember, your focus and purpose is the greater possession that the enemy can take from you. This day, let's ask God to fortify our vision and help us resist the distractions that lead us away from His will.

Contradictory winds are designed to silence the glory of God in our lives. In Mark 4:37, we see Jesus rebuke the wind, illustrating that we have the authority to confront these spirits directly. When storms arise, they come to silence our testimonies and destroy our peace. We must respond with faith, rebuking the winds and declaring the power of God over our situations.

Prayer Points

1. Against Spiritual Winds: Lord, we declare that every evil wind sent to disrupt our lives is nullified in the name of Jesus. We command the winds of adversity to cease and be still.

2. For Focus and Clarity: Father, help us focus on Your life's purpose. Strengthen our resolve against distractions that seek to steal our joy and peace.

3. For Protection of Possessions: We pray for the protection of our health, finances, and relationships. May nothing be taken from us that belongs to us according to Your will.

4. For Authority and Power: We ask for the boldness to confront every spiritual force that opposes us. May we walk in the authority You have given us as children of God.

DAY 15

WALKING IN SPIRITUAL AUTHORITY AND DISCERNMENT

Scripture Reading: Matthew 6:9-10; Psalm 91:11 TPT; 1 Kings 22:20-23 TLB

In our spiritual journey, the reality of prayer and worship is often intertwined, with worship serving as the vital key to unlocking the doors of heaven. As we reflect on our prayer lives, we must acknowledge the importance of praise. Psalm 100:4 reminds us that praise is not merely a formality but a password that grants us access to the very presence of God. If our worship is dry, it will invariably render our prayers ineffective.

Daniel's prayer in Daniel 9 reveals a profound pattern that can guide us in our spiritual engagements: praise, confession, and petition. Each stage is crucial; neglecting any part can weaken prayer life. Today, let us commit to being spiritually desperate for God's power as we pray for the full manifestation of His glory in our lives. We declare that as we walk in His authority, any forces of darkness that rise against us will crumble in His presence.

The world we inhabit often conditions us to equate usefulness with power. Psalm 37:10 states, "For yet a little while, and the wicked shall be no more." To lack power is to be rendered ineffective in our calling. It takes spiritual authority to overturn obstacles, defeat adversaries, and fulfill God's purpose for our lives. As we seek this power, we must understand the dynamic interplay between angels and demons in the spiritual realm.

1 Kings 22 narrates an account where God orchestrated events through His heavenly council to fulfill His purpose. Although a descendant of David, Ahab succumbed to a lying spirit, highlighting the importance of discernment. Just as God allowed a lying spirit to influence Ahab, we must be cautious of the voices we entertain in our lives. These influences can redirect us from God's will and position us for calamity.

In our quest for spiritual authority, we must recognize that our proximity to God defines our power in the spirit realm. Psalm 91:11 reassures us that God gives His angels a charge over us. However, when we neglect prayer, we demobilize our angelic protection. This is why we must be vigilant and intentional in prayer, consistently aligning ourselves with God's will.

Consider the case of Donald Trump, where our intercession played a pivotal role in diverting danger. This scenario is a stark reminder of our prayers' impact on the spiritual realm. As Church On Fire International members, our prayers have shifted atmospheres and changed destinies. Our authority is rooted in our relationship with God and the alignment of our hearts with His purposes.

Reflection: Are you aware of the spiritual battles surrounding your life? How often do you take time to discern the influences that affect your decisions? Today, evaluate the voices you listen to and the company you keep. Surround yourself with those who honor and respect God.

Let us remain vigilant against the tactics of the enemy, who seeks to misidentify us and attack our spiritual identity. The deceptive winds of life may try to disorient us, but we can rise against them through prayer and discernment.

I declare that any wrong identity I carry in the spirit realm that makes me a target for the enemy will be uprooted by the power of the Holy Spirit. I will walk in divine authority and not be a victim of satanic attacks. I align myself with God's purpose and will not be a substitute for evil.

Prayer Points

1. Lord, help me to understand the power of my praise and worship.
2. I pray for the discernment to recognize and reject any negative influences in my life.
3. Father, empower me to walk in authority over every spiritual adversary.
4. I declare that I and my family will not fall prey to the enemy's attacks.
5. May every lying spirit attempting to mislead me be silenced in Jesus' name.
6. Lord, align my heart with those who respect and honor You, guiding me in my relationships.

DAY 16

EMBRACING THE MYSTERY OF ETERNAL LIFE WITH CHRIST JESUS

Scripture Focus:
Philippians 2:13 (KJV) - "For it is God which worketh in you both to will and to do of his good pleasure."

As Believers are not merely participants in a religious system; we are co-heirs with Christ, invited into an eternal relationship that transforms our present and future. The Spirit of God desires to take us into irrevocable and irreversible possibilities, where the abstract becomes concrete and the intangible becomes tangible.

Reflect on the times you have been lifted into the Spirit

and encountered realities beyond your comprehension. These moments often leave us in awe, yet they also come with a vital call to action: to listen and obey God's specific instructions. Our hope, grounded in faith, must not remain abstract; it should manifest as substance in our lives. As Romans 8:24 tells us, "For we were saved in this hope; but hope that is seen is not hope." When we step into the reality of what God has shown us, our hope transforms into a living reality.

During one significant service, the Lord said, "What you want is wine; what you have is water." This profound revelation reminds many believers that they miss God during pivotal kairos moments. God desires to see us bring our 'water'—our offerings, sacrifices, and obedience—to the very brim. When we obey, even when it feels uncomfortable, we unlock the potential for divine overflow.

To truly walk with God, we must understand that obedience sometimes feels like choking. In these difficult moments, our pursuit of life must shift from seeking our desires to aligning with God's will. This trust in God allows us to transcend fear, which can lead to a life of wasted potential. Jesus cautioned us against living a life controlled by fear, for it can keep us trapped in spiritual paralysis.

As we go through life, we may find ourselves at the brink of our breakthroughs, looking at our pot and feeling satisfied. But God challenges us to consider: is there a lack of obedience between us and our greatness? Are we willing to fill our pots with obedience and faith?

God often requires our participation in His miracles. Every time He calls us to give, whether through time, talent, counsel, or financial contributions, He invites us to move from a position of lack to one of abundance. This co-creative partnership with God delights His heart. When we understand this, we begin to see the potential within us to change the world.

In moments of urgency, like when you felt the call to act on a generous impulse, remember that God is watching to see if you will respond. Your obedience creates a ripple effect, unlocking blessings not just for yourself, but for others. When you step out in faith, even if it feels inadequate, you partner with God to bring miracles.

As we conclude today's reflection, let us lift our voices in gratitude. Thank God for guiding us to understand, interpret, and align with His expectations. Pray that He helps us embrace the law of total abandonment, entrusting Him with our minds, hearts, and lives. May we fully surrender our fears and doubts, knowing that even while we sleep, God is at work, providing for His lovers.

Prayer Points

1. Thank God for His unwavering support and guidance in your life.
2. Ask Him for the strength to fill your life with obedience and to recognize the potential within you.
3. Pray for a greater understanding of your partnership with Him so that you may live as a co-creator in His divine plan.

Reflection Questions

1. In what areas of your life is God calling you to fill the pot to the brim?
2. How can you better respond to God's instructions, even when they challenge you?
3. What does it mean for you to co-create with God in your daily life?

Let today be a reminder that you are not merely existing; you are thriving in the mystery of eternal life with Christ Jesus, filled with hope and purpose.

DAY 17

THE POWER OF
WARRING ANGELS

Scripture Reading: Daniel 10:10-13 TLB

We often overlook the incredible forces in the unseen realm in our spiritual journey. Today, we look into the profound role of angels, specifically the warring angels assigned by God to protect and defend His people. Reflecting on Daniel's experience, we see that spiritual warfare is real and powerful. Daniel prayed earnestly, seeking answers, and though his prayer was heard immediately, the response was delayed due to opposition from wicked spiritual forces. This teaches us that while we may not always see the immediate results of our prayers, God is at work behind the scenes.

Both divine and demonic powers influence the world. Just as there are angels of light, there are also fallen angels working to thwart God's plans. In Daniel's case, a warring angel was sent to combat the opposition, ensuring that the answer to Daniel's prayer reached him. This illustrates the importance of prayer and the need for divine intervention in our lives.

As we pray today, let us focus on those in positions of influence, politically, financially, and socially, who may be working against God's kingdom. We declare that every man and woman occupying any position in this nation or around the globe who is working with darkness and demonic powers to keep God out shall be chased out! Let warring angels be released to torment and persecute them. We ask God to make their paths slippery and fill their surroundings with darkness. May the angels of God be assigned to those who seek power from evil sources, disrupting their plans and establishing God's authority.

The Lord assures us that our prayers hold power. We are not powerless in the face of evil; instead, we are called to be warriors in His army. As we align ourselves with God's purpose, we can dismantle the enemy's schemes. Let us remember that our position in Christ grants us authority over all spiritual forces. The enemy may try to intimidate us, but we stand firm in the knowledge of who we are in Him.

In our prayers, we declare: "Every wicked angel blocking our answers, promotions, positions, and prosperity, we arrest you now! Your assignment shall fail. We claim victory in Jesus' name."

The Mystery Of Angels

Angels serve various functions within God's kingdom. They are categorized in different orders, including:

Seraphim: The highest order of angels, who serve as throne angels and worship leaders.
Cherubim: Assistants to the Seraphim.
Throne Angels: Connected to God's judgment, mercy, and authority.

Dominions: Oversee the affairs of men.

Powers: Warrior angels who fight for God's people and protect them.

Among these, we find angels of virtue, such as Raphael, who is known for healing. These angels distribute God's gifts, healing, deliverance, miracles, and signs.

As we move forward, let us engage with the spiritual realm through prayer. Remember that our prayers not only impact our lives but also influence the world around us. We have the authority to call upon God's warring angels to fight on our behalf. In moments of spiritual opposition, declare the name of Jesus and remind the enemy of your identity in Christ.

Prayer For The Day

Heavenly Father, thank You for the angels You have assigned to protect and guide us. We stand in agreement today, declaring that every wicked influence attempting to rise against Your people shall be dismantled. We release Your warring angels to engage in battle on our behalf. Empower us to recognize our authority in Christ and to walk in victory, knowing that the battle belongs to You. In Jesus' name, we pray. Amen.

Let us embrace this truth: we are not fighting for victory but from victory, for our God is mighty, and His plans will prevail!

DAY 18

MASTERING THE ART OF CAPTURING DREAMS

Scripture Reference:
Joel 2:28 KJV - "And it shall come to pass afterward, that I will pour out my Spirit upon all flesh; and your sons and your daughters shall prophesy, your old men shall dream dreams, your young men shall see visions."

Dreams hold the power to inspire, challenge, and direct our lives. However, dreams are not always as fulfilling when they are stolen or left unguarded. As dreamers, it is crucial to master the art of capturing our dreams and visions. Failing to do so can result in losing the very essence of what God has placed in our hearts.

Matthew 20:16 (MSG) teaches us that we must cultivate an insatiable appetite for God's presence and purpose. This appetite promotes discipline and leads us to pursue our dreams without succumbing to the allure of immediate gratification. Many people desire grand visions and lofty ambitions, yet they falter when faced with the delay of their desires. Adam, for instance, experienced a life filled with perfection, yet he was still deceived into losing it all. This highlights that regardless of how ideal our circumstances may seem, vigilance is required.

Every vision and dream we harbor has the potential to resonate beyond our immediate reality, influencing the atmosphere around us. However, this also means that, if not protected, our dreams can become vulnerable to spiritual theft. We are reminded that there are forces that thrive on stealing the energy of our aspirations. They lurk in environments filled with divination and dark practices, waiting to siphon off the vitality of our visions.

As believers, we must recognize that the spaces we inhabit can either energize or drain our dreams. When we enter environments buzzing with ambition and creativity, we may find our dreams invigorated. Yet, without a protective shield, we risk the possibility of those dreams being manipulated or extinguished.

The urgency of retaining our dreams is vital, as demonstrated by the analogy of a phone with a drained battery. Even when a phone is powered down, its potential remains dormant until it is recharged. Similarly, we must remain plugged into God's source of energy to keep our aspirations alive and vibrant.

Unfortunately, many fail to heed the significance of clear spiritual instructions. A casual approach to guidance often leads to a lack of divine intervention. This is why we must stay attuned to God's voice, as it empowers us to activate our dreams. When we enter new atmospheres, it is essential to remember that our aspirations are not merely personal—they are intended to connect us with divine purpose.

Energy is crucial for attraction and sustainability. Ephesians 3:20-21 (TPT) reminds us that the true essence of God's power is energy, that is, a force that propels us forward. This energy can help us attract the right relationships, yet we must cultivate our inner strength to maintain them. Those who lack this sustainability often attract and repel the very people they need to help them achieve greatness.

Reflect on the people in your life. Do they elevate your energy and aspirations, or do they drain you? Surround yourself with individuals who reflect the vibrancy of your destiny, for their energy will enhance your journey.

Today, evaluate the environments you frequent and the relationships you cultivate. Are they conducive to your dreams, or are they filled with negativity? Recognize the beauty of your dreams and take action to guard them against theft. As you do, you will find your aspirations not only realized but thriving, producing fruitfulness in this season of your life.

Prayer Points

1. Lord, help me capture and guard my dreams. Let me not be careless with the visions You have given me.
2. Father, surround me with people who will energize and uplift my spirit. Guide me to relationships that reflect Your purpose for my life.
3. God, grant me the discipline to stay connected to Your source of strength so that my dreams remain alive and powerful.
4. In the name of Jesus, I rebuke any spirit of divination seeking to steal my dreams. I claim protection over my aspirations.
5. Holy Spirit, awaken my appetite for Your presence. Help me pursue my dreams with relentless passion and dedication.

DAY 19

THE POWER OF
MULTIPLYING
YOUR FRUITS

Scripture for Reflection:
"Blessed is the man who walks not in the counsel of the ungodly, nor stands in the path of sinners, nor sits in the seat of the scornful; but his delight is in the law of the Lord, and in His law he meditates day and night. He shall be like a tree planted by the rivers of water, that brings forth its fruit in its season, whose leaf also shall not wither; and whatever he does shall prosper."
Psalm 1:1-3 (TPT)

As believers, God calls us to bear fruit and not just any fruit, but fruit that will last. Your success, your spiritual growth, and your impact on the world should not be temporary. As Psalm 1:1-3 encourages, we must plant ourselves by the rivers of living water (the Word of God) and commit ourselves to being productive and fruitful in all areas of life. This fruit must remain, making a lasting difference for generations to come.

To bear fruit that lasts, we must dig deeper into God's word and refuse to settle for shallow victories or temporary success. Don't wait for magical solutions, or expect money to just fall into your lap without understanding how it works. Be intentional about going deep in your spiritual and practical endeavors. When God sees that you are committed to depth, He will take you deeper.

Reflection

Are you positioning yourself to produce lasting fruit, or are you content with temporary gains? God desires for you to multiply your impact and success, and it starts with cultivating a heart that is good. A heart that is filled with love, faith, and dedication will lead to results that cannot be easily erased. When your heart is right, your fruits will multiply and your influence will grow.

What Helps To Bring Forth Fruit That Lasts?

1. A Good Heart: If your heart is not in the right place, your fruit will not last. Position yourself by committing to growth and multiplying your efforts. Never settle for isolated success, expand your influence and reach.

2. Right Mindset: Your mindset determines your life's trajectory. Develop a champion's mindset that believes in long-term success. Develop the brave heart of a lion and the sharp eyes of an eagle. Be bold and courageous, seeing opportunities where others see obstacles. Proverbs 31:12 shows us the virtuous woman had many sources of income, she multiplied her impact and influence.

3. Vision and Capacity: Vision doesn't cost anything; it only requires imagination and faith. God will not give you more than

your capacity can handle. He wants you to grow organically, building the strength to carry what He entrusts to you. It takes a lion's heart to secure a lion's share. Believe in your capacity to steward greatness.

Prayer Points

1. Lord, help me to bear fruit that will last and impact generations.
2. Give me the wisdom and grace to expand my influence, multiplying my success in ways that glorify You.
3. Father, grant me a good heart and a strong mindset so I can fulfill the purpose You have for my life.
4. Let my vision be clear and my capacity strengthened to handle the blessings and responsibilities You are giving me.
5. I declare that my efforts will not fade, and my success will be rooted in You, bringing eternal results.

Prophetic Declaration

Today, I prophesy that your fruit will multiply, and your success will not be isolated or temporary. You will be like a tree planted by the rivers of water, bearing fruit in every season. The seeds you plant in this season will yield a harvest that lasts for generations. Every effort you make will prosper, and God will increase your capacity to handle more. You are stepping into a season of multiplied impact, God will give you the boldness to pursue greatness, and the results will speak for themselves.

DAY 20

BREAKING THE
CHAINS OF A
CORRUPTED SOUL

Scripture Reading: Matthew 18:33, Galatians 5:9, 1 Corinthians 11:1

When you gave your life to Christ, you asked Him to be the Lord over your soul, expelling the devil and his cohorts. However, allowing wickedness to grow in your heart is like inviting back an evil ex into your life. No matter how good Jesus is to your soul, if you allow darkness to fester, it will hinder your future.

The enemy knows how to use your past to sabotage your future. Wickedness, bitterness, and unforgiveness can corrupt your soul, attracting evil spirits and eventually leading to destruction. Even though many Christians outwardly profess their faith, their souls remain tainted with envy, manipulation, and competition. This corruption often manifests in subtle ways, such as when prayer partners pray for breakthroughs but secretly harbor doubt or jealousy.

Matthew 18:33 challenges us to show mercy as we have received mercy. Many Christians today find strength in tearing others down rather than building them up. This corrupt behavior is like a little leaven that spoils the whole lump (Galatians 5:9). It starts small but grows until it consumes your entire being, leading to spiritual downfall.

The truth is, when a person's heart is filled with corruption, even those closest to them can become enemies of their progress. They will be the first to bring them down when success comes. Instead of celebrating with them, they might attempt to compete, thinking they should always be on the same level. This mindset is dangerous and breeds division in the Body of Christ.

For revival to truly sweep through the church, this corruption must be dealt with. We often pray for God to change the world, but do we sincerely desire change for His glory or for our own comfort? A true heart for revival seeks God's glory above personal gain. Like a child who cleans their parent's home out of love, we should desire to see the church and the world transformed for God's sake.

If we approach our spiritual growth with selfish motives, focusing on our own comfort, our hearts will remain cold. But when we focus on the Father's passion, asking Him to change the world for His glory, He will move powerfully through us. This is when God begins to use us for His Kingdom purposes.

Satan is a master of sowing seeds of division in the church. One of his tactics is to make believers feel that others are competing with them, especially when they see someone else excelling in an area where they once thrived. This creates an unhealthy atmosphere of comparison, where we start to view others as rivals instead of fellow workers in the Kingdom.

1 Corinthians 11:1 teaches us to follow Christ and be an example for others to follow. Paul encouraged others to follow him as he followed Christ. Instead of being threatened by someone else's growth, we should help them rise even higher.

God is calling us to greatness, but we must do so with a heart of humility and grace. Greatness in the Kingdom is not about holding a position but continually rising and improving. The only way to secure your place is to keep growing, learning, and becoming better.

God wants us to have a competitive spirit, but one rooted in excellence, not in comparison. We compete to fulfill our purpose, not to outdo others. The Kingdom is not about arriving at a certain place and stopping; it is about continually ascending, getting better, and glorifying God with every step.

Prayer Points

1. Lord, purify my heart from any wickedness or corruption that hinders my relationship with You.
2. Help me to celebrate the success of others and contribute positively to the Body of Christ.
3. Father, give me a competitive spirit, not rooted in comparison, but in fulfilling Your purpose for my life.
4. I declare that I will continually rise, get better, and glorify You with my life.
5. Lord, let Your revival start in me. Transform my heart and use me for Your glory.

DAY 21

GUARDING YOUR
SPIRIT FOR
TRANSFORMATION

Scripture Reading: Proverbs 4:23, 1 Samuel 30:8, Luke 9:34-35

In our journey of faith, we are called to guard our hearts and minds diligently. Proverbs 4:23 reminds us that we must protect our hearts, for they are the wellspring of life. Every thought, emotion, and desire originates from our hearts, influencing our actions and spiritual state. If we allow negativity, doubt, and fear to infiltrate our hearts, we become vulnerable to the enemy's attacks, ultimately hindering our spiritual growth and effectiveness.

The days we live in are filled with both challenges and opportunities for spiritual transformation. God is calling us to deepen our spirituality while sharpening our discernment. The enemy seeks to distract us, leading our minds to wander and our hearts to doubt. We must stay vigilant, recognizing that spiritual hibernation can lead to careless living. As we navigate the complexities of life, we must continually inquire of the Lord, seeking His guidance and wisdom.

1 Samuel 30:8 illustrates the importance of seeking God's direction. David inquired of the Lord during a crisis, and God provided clear instruction. Similarly, we must develop a habit of asking questions, asking God about our paths, plans, and even the strategies of the enemy. When we actively seek God's guidance, we open ourselves to His divine wisdom and protection. Rather than wallowing in past failures, let us focus on how we can grow and strengthen our faith.

As we pursue a deeper relationship with God, we should also strengthen our spiritual mantle. Each time we come together as a body of believers, let us approach with the mindset of a leader, prepared to be equipped and empowered to impact the nations. Your presence in church is not just about attending; it's about accepting the call to be God's voice and light in the world.

God has anointed you for greatness, just as He poured oil over David, marking him for leadership. The world is waiting for you to rise and shine. When you embrace your calling, you become a force to be reckoned with. Deuteronomy 34:9 reminds us that the spirit of wisdom and understanding was transferred to Joshua. Likewise, God is equipping you to carry His glory and speak His truth to the nations.

In Luke 9:34-35, we see that when Jesus prayed, the glory of God manifested, and His voice was heard. God is ready to confirm and affirm your calling, but you must be attuned to His voice. He wants to reveal the depths of His purpose for you. You are not just a passive participant in God's plan; you are an active player, chosen to be His ambassador.

To effectively fulfill your calling, you must master the art of God-crafting. This involves understanding that everything around you, both seen and unseen, can serve as a tool in God's hands for your destiny. When you grasp this, you will become equipped to deploy the abilities and possibilities that God has placed within you.

Evangelism and discipleship go hand in hand. While evangelism brings people to Christ, discipleship nurtures their growth in faith. You must train yourself in both areas. Take time to sharpen your skills, learn how to share the gospel effectively, and embody the love of Christ in your actions. This commitment will position you as a radical disciple-maker, influencing the world around you for God's glory.

Prayer Points

1. Lord, help me guard my heart and mind against distractions and negativity that can lead me away from You.
2. I ask for the wisdom to inquire of You in every aspect of my life and the faith to follow Your guidance.
3. Father, empower me to embrace my calling as a leader and voice for You in the nations.
4. Teach me to master the art of God-crafting, using every tool at my disposal to fulfill Your destiny for my life.
5. Lord, let my life reflect Your glory, and may I be a catalyst for transformation in my community and beyond.

DAY 22

THE POWER OF CONSECRATION

Scripture Reading: Exodus 28:2, Romans 8:13, Colossians 3:9

Consecration is one of the most powerful keys to living a victorious Christian life. It signifies the act of setting oneself apart for God, fully dedicating one's life to His purpose. When we choose consecration, we are intentionally walking away from everything that dishonors God and hinders our destiny. Exodus 28:2 highlights how God instructed garments of glory and beauty for the consecrated priests. This teaches us that when we consecrate ourselves, we allow God to clothe us in His glory and beauty, preparing us for service in His kingdom.

Consecration requires a deliberate commitment to holiness. It's a call to refuse the distractions and temptations of this world, choosing instead to focus on God's purpose. When God calls for consecration, He is inviting us to step into a higher level of spiritual responsibility. The world may hunt for sin, but those who are consecrated actively flee from it, choosing righteousness over rebellion.

Romans 8:13 in The Passion Translation tells us, "If you live controlled by the flesh, you are about to die. But if the life of the Spirit puts to death the corrupt ways of the flesh, we then taste His abundant life." Consecration means putting to death the sinful nature within us and allowing the Spirit of God to lead. Sin hunts for a few, but many chase after sin, entangled in its snares.

Sometimes, when we make mistakes, guilt and shame take over. Instead of confessing and moving forward, we dwell in guilt, which then fuels spiritual pride. This pride convinces us that we cannot return to God, even though His mercies are new every morning. But consecration teaches us to refuse these lies of the enemy. Instead, we must connect with God's power until we become fully aligned with His will.

When we consecrate ourselves, we align with our true identity in Christ. It is a rejection of the false identities imposed by sin. Romans 13:14 reminds us, "But put on the Lord Jesus Christ, and make no provision for the flesh, to fulfill its lusts." Consecration is more than just abstaining from sin; it is about putting on Christ and living in His righteousness.

Sexual sin and impurity are often among the greatest challenges faced by believers. Many confuse their desires with license, thinking that because they like something, they have permission to indulge. However, the truth is that our likeness for something does not give us a license for it. Impurity dominates a person, making them live as slaves to sin. But when we consecrate ourselves, we break the chains of impurity and live as children of God, free to walk in righteousness.

When your prayer life dies, your victory dies with it. The moment we stop engaging with God, we lose the spiritual power that sustains us. Consecration revives our prayer life, ensuring that we remain connected to God's strength. It is through prayer that we tap into the grace to resist sin and maintain our purity. Purity, in turn, brings power to the Church and the Body of Christ.

As Colossians 3:9 reminds us, we must "put off the old man with his deeds." The old nature, dominated by sin, must be cast off so that we can put on the new man, created in the likeness of Christ. The Church's power is restored when we, as believers, commit to personal and corporate consecration.

Prayer Points

1. Father, in the name of Jesus, as we consecrate ourselves to You, we reject every filthy garment and put off the old man.
2. Lord, clothe us in Your righteousness and empower us to walk in purity and holiness.
3. We command every spirit of impurity to be broken, and we declare that we are free from the power of sin.
4. Father, let every spiritual contradiction, warfare, sickness, disease, and stagnation, grow weaker and weaker in our lives as we walk in Your holiness.
5. Lord, strengthen our prayer lives and let Your power be manifest in us as we live in consecration to You.

DAY 23

GUARDING THE PROSPERITY OF YOUR SOUL

Scripture Reading: Psalms 124:7, Mark 8:36, Philippians 4:6

The soul is the most precious part of a person. Psalms 124:7 tells us, "Our soul is escaped as a bird out of the snare of the fowlers: the snare is broken, and we are escaped." This verse captures the battle for our soul, as the enemy's ultimate goal is to arrest it. He may influence areas of our lives, but his final target is always the soul, for it is the control valve of our entire existence. Your soul is where your will, emotions, and intellect reside, and it governs your connection to this world. Your spirit connects with God, but your soul relates to your body and the earth.

Mark 8:36 warns, "What good is it for someone to gain the whole world, yet forfeit their soul?" The greatest worth of a man is his soul, and nothing in this world can compensate for its loss. Your soul's prosperity determines the quality of your life on earth and your eternal destiny. This is why it is critical to guard your soul from influences that seek to weaken or corrupt it.

Your soul is where your thoughts are formed, and your life is a direct reflection of the quality of your thoughts. Proverbs 23:6-9 teaches us, "For as he thinketh in his heart, so is he." If you allow shallow or negative thoughts to dominate, your life will follow that direction. Shallow thinkers may win by mistake, but they will always lose by correction. To live a life of victory, you must develop a mind that is filled with purposeful, godly thoughts.

Worry is one of the worst forms of thinking. It is essentially man trying to solve God's problem, leading to anxiety. Philippians 4:6 reminds us to "Be anxious for nothing, but in everything by prayer and supplication, with thanksgiving, let your requests be made known to God." Worry and anxiety open the door to spiritual warfare, as demons thrive in environments of fear and doubt. When you worry, you are essentially leaving your soul vulnerable to attacks from the enemy.

1 Peter 5:7 encourages us to "Cast all your cares upon Him, for He cares for you." When we choose to carry our own burdens, we become weary, and this weariness often leads to depression. Depression, in turn, opens the door for spiritual oppression. The spirit of bondage cannot arrest a person unless they first succumb to the weight of depression. Daniel 7:25 reveals the enemy's strategy: to "wear out the saints." If we allow our minds to be consumed by worry and anxiety, we will find ourselves spiritually exhausted, making it easier for the enemy to attack.

Intentionally take your worries to God. Refuse to allow them to linger in your mind and open the door to further spiritual battles. As you bring your burdens to the Lord in prayer, do so with thanksgiving, trusting that He will handle what you cannot.

Your mind serves two primary functions: memory and

imagination. The enemy often tries to use your memories to bring up past hurts, failures, and negative experiences. However, your imagination is the tool God has given you to envision a future filled with hope. When your memory throws up darkness, allow your imagination to paint a picture of brightness and possibility. The future can transform your past, making even the darkest moments seem like stepping stones to your destiny.

Matthew 15:19 warns us about the thoughts that come from an impure heart: "evil ideas, murderous thoughts, adultery, sexual immorality, theft, lies, and slander." These are the things that pollute the soul and hinder your spiritual growth. Guard your thoughts, because your life is a product of them.

Prayer Points

1. Father, in the name of Jesus, I declare that my soul is free from the snares of the enemy, and I will not allow worry and anxiety to dominate my thoughts.
2. Lord, help me to cast all my cares on You, knowing that You care for me and will handle every concern.
3. Father, purify my heart and mind from any negative memories that the enemy may use to bring me down. Help me to focus on the future You have planned for me.
4. I declare that my thoughts will be aligned with Your Word, and my soul will prosper as I fix my mind on You.
5. Lord, as my soul prospers, let every area of my life flourish and reflect Your glory.

DAY 24

REWARDS OF LABOR
IN GOD'S KINGDOM

Scripture Reading: Hebrews 6:9-12, John 15:16, Matthew 5:8

God is not unjust. He never forgets your labor of love and service to others, especially to those who are fellow believers. Hebrews 6:9-12 encourages us that "God won't forget what you've done... your labor to your fellow needy Christians." God considers it an act of injustice to overlook the work and effort you've put into helping others, as it is ultimately a demonstration of love toward Him.

When we show love to the brethren, we are showing love towards God Himself. However, it is not enough to simply bring people to Christ; we must help them stay with Him. One of Satan's most focused efforts is not only keeping people away from faith but also causing those in the faith to backslide. He works harder to make people turn away from Christ than to prevent them from initially coming to Him.

John 15:16 reminds us of our purpose: "Ye have not chosen me, but I have chosen you, and ordained you, that ye should go and bring forth fruit, and that your fruit should remain." God desires that we not only bear fruit but that our fruit remains. It is a continuation of service and commitment that gets the attention of God. Your labor in the kingdom must be an ongoing act of service. When love is your driving force, your rewards will be abundant. If you stay on course, you will receive everything promised to you.

However, be cautious about your attitude in service. Do not colonize the labor of God's kingdom by treating it as your endeavor. When murmuring or complaining invades your service, it poisons the purity of your work. Service to God must come from a place of joy and cheerfulness, without the burden of duty. This kind of service advances you in the kingdom of God and attracts His favor.

One of Satan's tactics is to make your heart grow dull and weary. When this happens, your sense of eternity diminishes, and you begin to lose sight of God's eternal reward. Matthew 5:8 says, "Blessed are the pure in heart, for they shall see God." A pure heart keeps you connected to God and His promises. When depression or discouragement sets in, it becomes a gateway for the enemy to steal your joy and your reward.

Even five minutes of depression can create months of negativity and setbacks. If you find yourself struggling with discouragement, it's essential to flush out whatever negative influences have entered your heart. Don't allow a brief moment of despair to affect your long-term service and reward in God's kingdom.

God's faithfulness is often revealed through the rewards we receive for our labor in His kingdom. As Hebrews 6:12 encourages, we should follow those who have obtained their reward through faith and patience so that we, too, can inspire others to persevere. Serving God with faith, patience, and endurance is crucial to preparing us to receive His promises.

What Are Some Of The Rewards Of Laboring Faithfully In God's Kingdom?

1. God Himself (Genesis 15:1) – The greatest reward is God Himself. He told Abraham, "I am your shield, your exceedingly great reward." God's presence and favor are the ultimate rewards for a life of faithful service.

2. Oil/Anointing – Serving in the kingdom brings anointing, which is God's empowerment for high performance. Anointing enables you to operate beyond your natural abilities.

3. Wisdom – God grants wisdom to those who serve Him diligently. High wisdom results in high performance, allowing you to make decisions that yield great results.

4. Health and Vitality – Faithful service brings divine health and strength. As you labor in His vineyard, God strengthens your body, ensuring you have the vitality to continue.

5. Hope (Romans 5:5) – Your service brings hope, which anchors your soul and keeps you moving forward despite challenges.

6. Longevity (Exodus 23:26) – Serving God ensures that your days are lengthened and your life is fruitful.

7. Favor and Profitable Connections – God opens doors of favor for those who serve Him faithfully. This favor results in connections that bring joy, resources, and even marital blessings.

8. Joyful Service – Serving God cheerfully brings great rewards. Recognize that it is a privilege to labor in God's kingdom, and He will reward you with favor, joy, and blessings that will impact your life and those around you.

Prayer Points

1. Father, in the name of Jesus, thank You for being a just God who never forgets our labor of love. Help me to continue serving You with a pure heart.
2. Lord, my service will always be joyful and cheerful, free from murmuring or discouragement.
3. Father, help me to remain steadfast in my service, bearing fruit that remains for Your glory.
4. I receive the rewards of my labor in Your kingdom, including favor, health, wisdom, and divine connections.
5. Lord, may my heart remain pure and focused on You, so that I may see You and receive the fullness of Your promises.

DAY 25

SHARPENED BY GOD

Scripture Reading: 2 Samuel 11:1-4, Luke 14:17-24

To be effective, you must constantly sharpen yourself in God's presence. The sharper you are, the more impactful you become in fulfilling your purpose. As believers, we need God to continuously sharpen us mentally and spiritually to avoid becoming victims of the blessings He bestows upon us. Often, what was meant to be a blessing can become a stumbling block if we are not careful.

We should pray, "Lord, help me never to become a victim of your blessings. Help me not to fall into the trap of success or the good things you are doing in my life. Letting what you have given me as an asset is not why I backslide."

One of the most significant challenges believers face is the tendency to forget their spiritual investment during seasons of blessing. It's easy to let our guard down when things are going well, but we must remain vigilant. Just one ounce of pleasure or indulgence can cause years of spiritual progress to slip away. Satan knows this and often waits for us at the mountaintops of life, not in the valleys. He knows that champions fight well in the valley, but when success and comfort are present on the mountain, they may become careless.

David's story in 2 Samuel 11:1-4 serves as a cautionary example. After a series of victories, David became complacent. Instead of being on the battlefield, where kings should be, he remained in his palace. His idleness led to his downfall with Bathsheba, proving that even the mightiest warriors can become victims of success if they are not sharp and alert.

Laziness is another trap that often ensues believers at the peak of their success. When we fail to sharpen our minds and feed our spirits, we allow spiritual laziness to take over. The result is wasted potential, where talent meets a lack of diligence, causing failure to marry destiny. As believers, we must not allow the things God is doing in our lives to trap us in complacency.

Luke 14:17-24 gives us insight into the importance of responding to God's prophetic call. When God calls, it is an opportunity to activate our destiny. However, many fail to respond because they become distracted by the blessings they've received. The banquet in this parable represents the invitation to deeper fellowship with God, yet many made excuses, prioritizing their personal affairs over God's invitation.

What is it that God has given you that could potentially pull you away from Him? We must be careful that the blessings we receive don't become a hindrance to our walk with God. Remember, whatever pulls you away from God, He can take away to refocus your heart. The blessings of God are tests. If we pass the test, God gives us the rest—He gives us more. But if we fail, we lose what we've gained.

To be sharp means to have a fine point and to be on target at every moment. It also means to be clearly defined, distinct, and strong, in contrast to dullness. Adam was once sharp. He operated with mental and spiritual sharpness, exercising dominion over all creation. The animals feared him because of his authority. But the moment he fell into the trap of disobedience, he became spiritually dull.

We should not allow our testimony to become our tragedy. Sometimes, God delays our testimony because He cannot trust our hearts. He knows that if we are not sharp, the blessings we receive will become weapons in the enemy's hands to destroy us. Satan wants us to be weak and ineffective, like worms, unable to fulfill God's purpose. But God is looking for those who will remain humble and sharp, even amid blessings.

The key to remaining sharp is humility. God is looking for humility in men, especially during times of weakness. In our humility, God can sharpen us and make us effective for His kingdom. When we remain sharp, everything we touch becomes impactful and significant. Our lives become distinct, clearly defined, and aligned with God's purpose.

Prayer Points

1. Father, sharpen me spiritually and mentally so I can be effective in my life and ministry.
2. Lord, protect me from becoming a victim of the blessings You've given me. Help me not to backslide or become complacent.
3. Father, help me pass every test You give me so that I may receive the fullness of Your blessings.
4. Lord, keep me sharp and alert, even in times of success and comfort. Help me to remain focused on You.
5. Father, grant me humility in all seasons of life so that I may remain valuable and practical for Your kingdom.

DAY 26

THE POWER
OF SPIRITUAL
SENSITIVITY

Scripture Reading: Matthew 13:16, John 20:21-27

If we are unaware of many things, Satan can easily use them to his advantage. He is skilled at using God's very purpose and plan for our lives against us. This is why spiritual sensitivity is critical. We must learn the principles that will birth God's purpose. Without this understanding, Satan can use our lack of knowledge to distract and derail us.

God desires us to develop a heightened sensitivity to His voice and His leading. This sensitivity comes through intimacy with Him. In Matthew 13:16, Jesus said, "But blessed are your eyes, for they see: and your ears, for they hear." Thomas, however, struggled with doubt and missed out on this intimacy. Despite being physically close to Jesus, he could not encounter the fullness of who Jesus was. He allowed his mind to be distracted and disconnected from the spiritual realities around him.

Satan often uses distractions to keep us from hearing and experiencing what God has for us. Sometimes, the distraction is external, a situation or challenge that pulls us away from focusing on God. Other times, it's internal, where our minds are present physically but not spiritually engaged. John 20:25 recounts how Thomas allowed doubt to dominate his heart even after hearing that Jesus had risen. His mind wasn't aligned with the spiritual reality unfolding before him. Because of this, he missed out on a significant encounter with Jesus.

How often have we been in God's presence but missed an encounter because our minds were elsewhere? It's possible to be physically present but mentally absent. When our minds wander, we cannot fully capture the reality of God's presence.

A wandering mind reflects in other areas of life. It makes the body tired, distracts us from the purpose, and can even hinder us from receiving what God has for us. When your mind is fully awake and engaged, your spirit responds, and you become spiritually alert. That's when you're able to receive direction from God. The days when your mind, heart, and spirit align are the days you are most likely to encounter God.

God uses His word to sharpen us and increase our spiritual sensitivity. To be sharp spiritually means to have the ability to discern things before they happen. It means picking up spiritual information and seeing into the future God has planned for you and His people. A sharp mind and spirit can seize opportunities because they can see them before they manifest. But it's hard to own a future you haven't seen.

In John 20:21-27, Jesus spoke to His disciples and commissioned them for their future ministry. Yet Thomas, who wasn't there, doubted the reality of Jesus' resurrection. His doubt was a sign of spiritual dullness. Thomas missed a robust commissioning because he wasn't present, both physically and spiritually.

God often shows us glimpses of the future through visions or words, but if our minds are wandering, we miss these revelations. When we allow intimacy with God to be interrupted, spiritual dullness sets in. This dullness makes it hard to hear or understand God's direction for our lives. Intimacy with God sharpens us, but when intimacy is scarce, so is clarity.

Intimacy with God gives us access to spiritual accuracy. The more intimate we are with Him, the clearer we hear His voice and understand His will. Thomas missed his opportunity to witness Jesus' commissioning because he wasn't there when it happened. Doubt crept in and clouded his ability to see the truth.

Our spiritual accuracy is determined by the depth of our intimacy with God. The closer we are to Him, the more attuned we become to His voice, and the more easily we can discern His plans for our lives. When we value closeness with God, we remain spiritually sharp, and our lives become aligned with His purpose.

Prayer Points

1. Father, sharpen my spiritual sensitivity so that I can clearly discern Your voice and direction in my life.
2. Lord, protect me from distractions that keep me from encountering Your presence and purpose.
3. Father, help me stay spiritually awake and alert, with my mind, heart, and spirit aligned with You.
4. Lord, draw me into deeper intimacy with You so that I may gain spiritual accuracy and clarity.
5. Father, help me to see and seize the future You have planned for me through divine revelation and discernment.

DAY 27

SHARPENED BY GOD'S FAVOR

Scripture Reading: Deuteronomy 15:6-9, Psalms 102:13

This week is a week of sharpening, and I subscribe fully to what God is doing in my life. The struggles of life often bring frustration, putting in much effort only to see little results. Many times, we pour our energy into life, yet the return seems disproportionate to our labor. This can feel overwhelming, but there is hope in God's promises.

Deuteronomy 15:6-9 reminds us of God's intention for His people to live in abundance and not lack. Success, as it is often said, has many relatives, and through God's favor, we can be drawn into places of abundance that human effort alone cannot reach. Proverbs 22:7 explains that it is not God's will for us to be enslaved to the limitations of struggle. His favor breaks the chains that hold us back and positions us for divine increase.

Favor is a multiplier. Where struggle diminishes, favor amplifies. Luke 6:38 teaches us that as we give, it shall be given to us in abundance, pressed down, shaken together, and running over. The measure of favor we receive from God turns even the slightest effort into something significant. This divine favor adds flavor to our lives, making everything we do fruitful and rewarding.

Psalm 23:5 shows us how God prepares a table before us, even in the presence of our enemies. Our challenges are transformed into opportunities for God to showcase His favor. Even the most challenging moments become occasions for God to demonstrate His goodness in our lives.

Ecclesiastes 10:10 speaks of the importance of being sharpened. When an ax is dull, much more strength is needed, but the work is accomplished with ease when sharpened. God does this for us when He sharpens our lives with His favor. He strengthens our vision, focuses our efforts, and adds divine grace to our work.

Genesis 39:21 and Luke 2:52 remind us of how God's favor positioned Joseph and Jesus for greatness. Wherever Joseph went, God's favor distinguished him, causing everything he touched to prosper. The same favor was upon Jesus, who grew in wisdom and stature and favor of both God and men. Favor opens doors, connects us to destiny helpers, and positions us for divine appointments.

How do we position ourselves for God's favor? Matthew 5:7 calls us to be merciful, for mercy attracts favor. Psalm 102:13 speaks of God arising to favor us in His set time. There is a divine timing for favor, and as we align ourselves with God's will, He ensures that those who carry what we need are drawn to us. Connections and opportunities that would have otherwise been missed become accessible through the sharpening of favor in our lives.

Prayer Points

1. Lord, sharpen my life with Your favor, allowing me to achieve more with less effort.
2. Father, position me for divine opportunities to showcase Your glory.
3. Let everyone who carries what I need locate me by Your divine favor.
4. Lord, sharpen my vision and focus so I may walk in the fullness of Your plan.
5. Your favor multiplies my efforts and brings abundant results.

When God sharpens our lives with His favor, every struggle is replaced with grace. The favor of God multiplies our efforts, connects us to the right people, and positions us for success beyond what we could achieve on our own. Embrace His favor today and watch as He sharpens every area of your life.

DAY 28

SHARPENED FOR CLARITY AND PRECISION

Scripture Reading: Isaiah 6:6-13, Mark 8:24

Spiritual things are meant to be clear and specific. When there is no clarity, confusion reigns, bringing along assumptions, frustration, stagnation, regression, and empty speculations. Speculation often leads to deprivation, as it prevents us from receiving the fullness of what God has prepared for us.

God desires to give us clarity and sharpness in every area of life. Ecclesiastes 10:15 explains how a lack of understanding can lead to weariness. When you are not sharp in your knowledge and spiritual discernment, your progress is slowed, and you risk becoming exhausted by life's challenges. Insisting on being sharp in spirit, mind, and actions helps you navigate life more effectively.

Confusion of the mind, eyes, and ears can derail your spiritual progress. Satan often uses these areas to prevent people from receiving God's word. When there is no understanding, it becomes easy to stand under the weight of things God never intended for us to carry. The enemy's goal is to make us weary and ineffective by distorting our ability to see, hear, and understand.

Mark 8:24 highlights how Jesus healed a man's vision, transforming blurry sight into clear vision. This physical healing is a powerful metaphor for spiritual clarity. God wants to sharpen our ability to see precisely, ensuring our spiritual journey is free from confusion. When we understand what God is doing, we gain confidence in following His lead.

A soul cluttered with bitterness, confusion, or assumptions becomes a tool in Satan's hands. Jesus solved people's problems by addressing the root causes in their hearts and souls. We open ourselves to confusion and distraction when we carry emotional wounds or refuse to purify our hearts.

The Bible emphasizes the importance of purity and fellowship with God. We must purify our souls and sharpen our spiritual senses to avoid confusion. God desires to remove the confusion from our eyes, ears, and minds. He calls us to submit ourselves to Him, allowing His Word to heal and sharpen us for greater effectiveness.

Sharpness is when you can put in less effort but command great results. Precision in your spiritual walk ensures that you avoid unnecessary toil and weariness. The enemy's strategy is to cause us to labor without fruit, leaving us weary and vulnerable. It's easy to defeat someone tired, but a sharp, focused believer is unstoppable.

Ecclesiastes 10:10 teaches that a sharpened ax makes work easier. God sharpens us through fellowship, teaching us His ways and equipping us to do His work precisely. When we embrace the Kingdom of God, we learn His principles and walk in His Lordship. This sharpness enables us to see clearly, hear accurately, and think wisely—all of which signal our spirit to align with God's will.

Fellowship with God sharpens your entire being. It brings you to a deeper place in Him, where clarity and precision become the norm. When you submit to God and come into His presence through the purifying blood of Jesus, your soul is sanctified, and your ability to hear and see is restored.

Isaiah 6:6-13 shows how Isaiah's encounter with God led to a sharpening of his prophetic call. His lips were touched by a burning coal, purifying him for the work ahead. Similarly, our fellowship with God refines us, purifies our thoughts, and aligns our spirit with His purpose. This fellowship is an invitation to step into a sharper, more precise walk with God.

Prayer Points

1. Lord, sharpen my ability to see, hear, and understand Your will with clarity and precision.
2. Father, remove any confusion from my life, purify my soul, and align me with Your purpose.
3. I declare that my spiritual senses are sharpened to navigate life with less effort and more significant results.
4. Lord, I submit to Your sharpening process, allowing You to purify and guide me in all things.
5. Let my fellowship with You deepen, bringing me clarity and spiritual sharpness.

When God sharpens us, He removes the confusion and assumptions that hinder our progress. As we embrace fellowship with the Father, our ability to see, hear, and understand with precision is restored. In this place of clarity, we can move forward confidently, trusting in God's guidance and provision.

DAY 29

STRENGTHENED
BY GOD'S MERCY
AND POWER

Scripture Reading: Psalm 68:28, Psalm 18:17-19, Habakkuk 3:2

In moments of weakness, the enemy is always ready to strike. Just as vultures wait for strong animals to grow weak before they attack, demons watch for moments of spiritual weakness when our prayer life, faith, or pursuit of God wanes. This is when the enemy launches his most aggressive attacks. Psalm 18:17-19 reminds us that the enemy does not attack us when we are strong but waits until we are most vulnerable. SCalling the Lord for strength and protection is vital in such moments. Salm 68:28 emphasizes that God's power is the source of our strength. We cannot rely on our abilities to sustain us during spiritual warfare. We must ask God to strengthen our lives, restore our faith, and help us rise when we feel weak. His power ensures the enemy cannot prevail over us in our most fragile state.

When we cry out for God's mercy, we invite His intervention in our lives, opening the door for miracles, signs, and wonders. His mighty power, displayed through our lives, reminds the enemy that we are not alone and that God is with us. His strength defeats the enemy and lifts us out of the pit of weakness.

Let Us Pray:

"Father, in the name of Jesus, by Your mercy and power, we ask that You do it again. We have heard of the mighty miracles, signs, and wonders You performed in times past. Lord, parade Your power once more in our lives, Church on Fire International, and every member's lives. Let the fire of revival burn in the souls of those connected to this family and beyond. Let it spread across the Chicagoland area, North America, and South America."

We pray for financial turnarounds, the fire of revival to ignite across communities and nations, and God's miraculous power to change lives. Habakkuk 3:2 reflects our cry for God to move in our time as He did in the old days.

"Father, in the name of Jesus, by Your mercy and authority, we ask for extreme mercy upon our lives, households, and communities. May Your mercy heal, strengthen, and restore us, shielding us from every enemy attack."

Relying on God's mercy and power strengthens us to stand firm against the enemy's attacks. Even in our weakest moments, His power is perfect, and His mercy sustains us. Let us trust in His strength and allow His mighty hand to work wonders in our lives.

DAY 30

REDEEMING TIME AND ALIGNING WITH GOD'S PURPOSE

Scripture Reading: John 5:5, Ephesians 5:15, Luke 10:38, Hebrews 4:12

In John 5:5, we see a man whose struggle was physical but also spiritual and mental. His real issue was not his disability but his heart and mindset. He blamed others for his situation and lived in a cycle of falsehood, convincing everyone, even himself, that he wanted to be healed. His biggest problem was not external; it was the internal condition of his heart.

This is a critical lesson for us: the state of your heart and mind is essential to your growth. When you're under pressure, the real you is revealed. If your mindset is full of excuses and self-pity, it steals your time and life, leading to stagnation. Ephesians 5:15

warns us to walk as wise, not foolish, redeeming our time because the days are evil.

Wisdom is displayed by how we value and use our time. Luke 10:38 tells the story of Mary, who sat at Jesus' feet, prioritizing learning and intimacy with God over the busyness of life. Mary chose the better part, and no one could take that away from her.

This teaches us that wise people focus on what truly matters: God's purpose. When we rightly prioritize our lives, we align ourselves with His will, and peace and courage fill us. John 14:27 assures us that God's peace is not the absence of crises but the strength and courage to face them confidently.

When you align with God's will, He reveals things others may overlook. Mary uncovered the secret of sitting in God's presence, while others missed it. When you make discoveries in God, you need little or no encouragement because you have encountered the truth that transforms your life.

Hebrews 4:12 reminds us that the word of God discerns our thoughts and reveals the true motives of our hearts. When your motives are pure, God can use you mightily. It is not enough to merely know God's will; you must apply your life to His purpose, adjusting your lifestyle to fit the demands of your calling.

Surrendering to the Word is like undergoing surgery. It cuts deep, revealing your innermost thoughts, motives, and intentions. Actual spiritual growth happens when you allow the Word to purify and sharpen your character. This is the redemption process —buying back time and investing it in the right things.

In life, whatever steals your time steals your life. When you invest your time wisely, focusing on God's purpose, you redeem the future. Buying time means investing it in what truly matters, things that no one can take away. Three hundred sixty-five days a year is one of the most significant opportunities for life redemption. When you wisely use God's time, you own the future.

Prayer Focus

Let us pray for wisdom, revelation, and alignment with God's purpose so that we may walk as wise, redeeming our time and growing in His grace daily.

DAY 31

THE MYSTERY OF KINGDOM GREATNESS

Scripture Reading: John 14:23, Revelation 3:18-19, Isaiah 54:14, Matthew 22:14

Every story of greatness in the Kingdom of God is intertwined with a mystery. From Genesis to Revelation, those who walked faithfully with God transitioned from zero to hero, from nothing to something, from non-entities to celebrities. Their journeys weren't merely personal tales; they became stories of legacy and trans-generational blessings.

Successful walking with God begins with a genuine heart that loves Him. A corrupt heart will always limit your relationship with the Almighty. Jesus promised in John 14:23 that the Father will love anyone who uniquely loves Him. This love isn't the general agape love that encompasses everyone. Instead, it's a more profound, intimate love reserved for those who genuinely desire a close relationship with God. While agape love is an invitation to all, it does not qualify one for friendship with God.

Many Christians attend church, sing, and shout praises but remain strangers to the heart of God. How can you tell if you're not a friend of God? When He doesn't share His secrets with you. Living without access to the mind of God leads to spiritual blindness. Revelation 3:18-19 warns that those who think they have sight may be blind.

Like Abraham, people who have walked closely with God were granted unique insight and attention. God even questioned, "Can I hide from my friend Abraham?" This shows us that those who cherish their relationship with God are privy to divine revelations. Ignoring or devaluing your relationship with God can lead to significant consequences.

For instance, an entire city was on the brink of destruction, and only Abraham, a friend of God, was informed. You risk missing vital information and blessings when you commonize essential relationships. Without a genuine friendship with God, your life lacks interpretation. All your battles and pains will seem meaningless until you cultivate a relationship with Him.

A loveless world is sightless, and spiritual blindness often stems from a lack of love for God. If you desire to see and understand God's purpose for your life, you must first develop a genuine passion for Him.

The initial love we receive from God is generic and invitational. However, as we deepen our relationship with Him, we gain insight into the more profound mysteries of the Kingdom. The Holy Spirit reveals God's secret things to those who love Him genuinely.

God has designed a system where He uses people to accomplish His purposes on earth. He doesn't intervene directly because He has entrusted the world to humanity. When Adam fell, God did not save him by directly intervening; instead, He set a plan in motion for those responding to His call.

God wants us to be robust and knowledgeable in His ways. Isaiah 54:14 promises that in this season, evil will be far from you. The wealth that is coming belongs to believers, not sinners. However, if you are unaware of what belongs to you, you will struggle to reclaim it.

Many believers are disadvantaged in the spiritual realm because they do not understand the principles governing their inheritance. Many are unaware of the spiritual attacks that occur at night when evil spirits are most active.

Sinners are often more dedicated to their pursuits than believers are to their spiritual responsibilities. This lack of dedication can hinder God from giving believers what He has promised. The principles that govern the earth are set, and God requires us to understand these systems.

You must connect with God's ways and thoughts to excel in life. Psalms 115:16 reminds us that we are in charge of the earth, but many fail to operate within the divine systems God has established. Understanding these systems, like the code of sacrifice mentioned in Hebrews 11:4, is crucial. It's not about the quantity of sacrifice but the quality and sincerity of your heart.

In this journey of faith, let us strive to develop a genuine love for God, seek His friendship, and understand the mysteries of His Kingdom. This will enable us to walk in authority, experience His blessings, and fulfill our divine purpose. May we commit to pursuing a deeper relationship with Him, becoming true friends of God who walk in wisdom and revelation.

Prayer Points

1. Prayer for a Genuine Heart: Lord, create a clean heart and renew my steadfast spirit. Help me to have a genuine love for You that

draws me closer to Your heart.

2. Prayer for Revelation: Father, I ask for the revelation of Your secrets. Open my eyes to see the mysteries of Your Kingdom and grant me access to Your mind and heartbeat.

3. Prayer for Spiritual Insight: Lord, let me not walk in spiritual blindness. Illuminate my path and help me to understand the systems and principles that govern Your creation.

4. Prayer for Friendship with God: Jesus, I desire to be Your friend. Teach me how to develop an intimate relationship with You to hear Your voice and understand Your plans for my life.

5. Prayer for Protection and Guidance: Heavenly Father, protect me from evil influences as I navigate life. Guide me to walk in Your ways and experience the blessings that belong to me as Your child.

6. Prayer for Boldness in Pursuing God's Promises: Lord, empower me to be bold and take hold of the promises You have for me. Help me diligently seek Your face and live according to Your will.

www.ingramcontent.com/pod-product-compliance
Lightning Source LLC
Chambersburg PA
CBHW071904020426
42331CB00010B/2655